HYMNS TO CHRIST
and a concert of miniatures

Original title: *Inni a Cristo e un concerto di miniature*. Published in Italy by
Edizioni Paoline. Copyright © Figlie di San Paolo, Roma 1981.

Edited by Costante Berselli

Iconographic research by M. Luisa Badenchini
Translated from the Italian by Sr Mary of Jesus O.D.C.

St Paul Publications
Middlegreen, Slough SL3 6BT, England

English translation copyright © St Paul Publications 1982
First published in Great Britain September 1982
Printed in Italy by Istituto Grafico Bertello, Borgo San Dalmazzo, 1982
ISBN 085439 210 6

*St Paul Publications is an activity of the priests
and brothers of the Society of St Paul who promote
the Christian message through the mass media*

Preface

In the month of November 1966, the River Arno, giving the lie to all the ancient titles bestowed on it in song, rose with unlooked-for fury, and caused devastation in Florence that time will not be able to obliterate.

The greatest victim of the flood, among an illustrious artistic patrimony, was a masterpiece of Cimabue, the most renowned painter of the twelfth century, the "Michelangelo of his age" and "the great patriarch of Italian painting". The Crucifixion, in the possession of the Museum of Santa Croce, painted on a wooden panel was disfigured and soiled by the muddy water; the colour was destroyed in varying degrees, damaging this great painting almost irreparably.

Patient work has accomplished the restoration so much desired by art lovers. But today, whoever looks at it must use a strong effort of memory to recapture the beauty of the original and perceive the inspiration of the master who has added to our religious and artistic patrimony an image of the crucified Redeemer which is "at the same time calm and yet pulsing with tragic violence".

A similar effort will be demanded of the reader of these hymns to Christ if he would capture, at the distance of so many centuries, the spirituality which entered into their recital during the first millennium of the Church.

The edict of the Emperor Diocletian at the beginning of the fourth century unleashed the fury of the last and worst of the persecutions, and demanded of the Christians to give up their sacred books to be destroyed.

For the persecutors, this meant not only the Bible, but all the texts used in cultic celebrations and for the readings during the Christian assemblies, comprising therefore the codices with letters, sermons and doctrinal tracts in the possession of the community of faithful.

The persecution of Diocletian raged over the whole area of the Empire and the destruction of books was such as to create an almost total void for the religious culture of the first three centuries. The greater part of the writings of the Apostolic Fathers such as Pope Clement, Ignatius of Antioch, Polycarp of Smyrna, were lost beyond recall, together with those of the first apologists such as Justin, the Christian philosopher and martyr, and the works of all the other writers who, as the Church expanded, had enriched the patrimony of the Church by their science and study.

The end of the era of persecutions did not see the end of the dispersion of the sacred texts, although the restoration of Western monasticism favoured the copying and a more careful preservation of the written doctrinal patrimony.

The complex political situation of the Empire, the barbarian invasions and the so-called Dark Ages were not propitious for the preservation of codices.

So the hymns presented in this volume are fragments, separate voices and isolated echoes of the mighty chorus of the Church of the first centuries.

There is enough left however to allow us to recapture the content and form of expression of the primordial Christian piety. The prayer to the Father, taught by Christ to his disciples, is interposed with the mediation of Jesus, the Saviour, and the cooperation of the Holy Spirit. Thus prayer becomes "trinitarian", rich in expression and revealing the personal mode of the one praying in manifesting his faith from the ambo in a church, or on the stake or in the circus before martyrdom.

Written in Syriac, Greek or Latin in words which have changed their original meaning, and in the syntactic structures created by the authors themselves, who were constrained to express ideas and doctrines hitherto unknown, it is not easy to translate them into modern idiom — their inspiration is expressed in a form too distant from our contemporary culture.

Yet these hymns are concise and solemn epitaphs carved in the still living traces of the ancient Church and lend themselves to interpretation and meditation.

They are presented in this book with a concert of miniatures which will help the reader to enter into the atmosphere of the "gloria" and "hosanna" repeated with such insistence by these hymns.

C. Berselli

The four illuminated codices

The miniatures used to illustrate the hymns to Christ are taken from a French codex belonging to the Cathedral of Albens and from three codices in the Biblioteca Estense in Modena.

PSALTER from the Library of the Chapter of Albens
Miniatures of the 13th century of the French School, executed for a monastery of northern France as is proved by the calendar and Litany of the saints added to the Psalter. The codex was gifted to the Cathedral of Albens in the first half of the 17th century. Hitherto unpublished, it is here printed for the first time, with initials and tail pieces representing biblical scenes.
Pages 11, 13, 15, 17, 19, 21, 23, 25, 27, 29, 31, 33, 35, 37, 39, 41, 43, 45, 47, 49, 51, 53, 55, 57.

GRADUAL (Lat. 1016)
Miniatures of the Bolognese School belonging to the end of the 13th and beginning of the 14th century with evident Byzantine influence. Those reproduced include: intial G with the crowning with thorns; initial M with St Agnes; initial G with heavenly glory; initial G with the risen Christ and Mary Magdalen; initial I with the story of St John; initial D with the apostles Peter and Paul; initial M with the scene at Emmaus; initial N with Peter being set free from prison; initial D with the calling of Peter and Andrew; initial L with the conversion of Saul; initial E with the martyrdom of Stephen; initial A with Christ in glory; initial L with the martyrdom and glorification of St Catherine.
Pages 61, 65, 69, 71, 75, 77, 83, 85, 87, 97, 99, 101, 107.

ANTIPHONARY (Lat. 1003)
Miniatures of the Bolognese School from the workshop of Nicolò di Giacomo (14th century). Two miniatures are reproduced: initial H with the adoration of the Magi and initial A with Christ in glory and nine prophets.
Pages 81, 89.

GRADUAL (Lat. 1005)
Miniatures of the Bolognese School belonging to the period between the end of the 13th century and the close of the 14th. We reproduce: initial B with Christ and two disciples; initial I with the episode at Emmaus; initial V with the Ascension; initial I with the temptation of Jesus; initial R with the Resurrection; initial C with Jesus Master and a young man; initial Q with the apostle Thomas and the risen Jesus; initial H with angels and shepherds; initial I with Jesus disputing with the Pharisees; initial D with Jesus in the garden of Gethsemane.
Pages 59, 63, 67, 73, 79, 91, 93, 95, 103, 105.

HYMNS TO CHRIST

The first Christian prayer

ather;
May your name be glorified;
Your kingdom come;
Give us day by day,
The bread by which we live;
Forgive us our sins;
As we forgive those who have sinned against us;
And do not allow us to be overcome by temptation.

Luke 11, 2-4

Initial S. The baptism of Jesus. The Father proclaims:
"This is my Son, the beloved. Hear him".

Invocations before martyrdom

et no creature, visible or invisible, attract me, so that I may belong to Jesus Christ alone.

Fire and the cross; herds of wild beasts; torn, stretched, rent, lacerated limbs; dislocated bones; crushed body; and all the tremendous torments of the devil let them all come upon me if only I can rest in Jesus Christ.

All the kingdoms of this world and the joy of them are nothing to me. I prefer to die in Christ than to reign from one end of the earth to the other.

I seek him who died for us; I long for him who rose again for our sakes.

Be good to me, my brothers; do not impede my birth into life, do not kill me [by preventing me from dying for Christ], do not give to the world one who desires to belong only to God. Allow me to turn to that pure light: when I arrive there [in the arena] I will be a man of God indeed.

Let me imitate the passion of my God. Let anyone who lives with God in his heart understand my desire, and sympathize with me in my torment.

Ignatius of Antioch

*The annunciation of the angel to Mary and
the visitation of Mary to Elizabeth.*

Prayer at the stake

e was not nailed but bound. And bound thus, with his hands behind his back, he seemed like a lamb chosen from the flock for the sacrifice, prepared as a holocaust pleasing to God; and raising his eyes to heaven he said:

Lord, God almighty, Father of Jesus Christ, your blessed and beloved Son who has taught us to know you.

God of the angels, of the whole of creation, of the whole race of the just who live in your presence: I bless you because you have judged me worthy of this day and of this hour; worthy to be added to the number of the martyrs; worthy to drink the chalice of your Christ, so as to rise up to eternal life in body and soul in the immortality of the Holy Spirit.

May I today be numbered among the martyrs in your presence as a precious and acceptable victim; bring to completion that which your will has prepared and revealed to me; God, faithful and true, for this grace and for all the others, I praise you, I glorify you, and bless you through our eternal heavenly priest, your beloved Son, Jesus Christ.

Through him, with him, and with the Holy Spirit, may you be glorified now and through all ages.
Amen.

Polycarp of Smyrna

*Birth of Jesus at Bethlehem
and the angels' announcement to the shepherds.*

Prayer to Christ

O Jesus, immaculate Lamb,
you are both father and mother;
my brother and my friend; . . .
You are he who is all, and that all is in me;
You are he who is, and nothing exists apart from you.

Take refuge in him, you too, my brothers;
and when you have understood that only in him will you have life,
then you will receive that joy that was promised:
"That which eye has not seen
nor ear heard,
nor has it entered into the heart of man to imagine".

Grant to us, then, what has been promised.

We praise you, we thank you, we bear witness to you;
we, weak mortals, give you glory,
you who alone are God, for there is no other.
Glory to you, now and to the end of time.
Amen.

Acts of Peter

The Magi on their way
and in adoration of Jesus in Mary's arms.

Offertory prayer

he grace of our Lord Jesus Christ, the love of God the Father and the fellowship of the Holy Spirit be with us all, now and for ever and through the ages! Amen.
Lift up your hearts!

— To you, God of Abraham, of Isaac, of Israel, O King of glory! The offering is made to God, the Lord of all things.

— It is right and praiseworthy so to do.

It is right that every tongue should glorify, every voice attest, every creature venerate and celebrate the adorable and glorious name of the most holy Trinity, Father, Son and Holy Spirit, who created the world in their loving kindness and out of their goodness saved men and granted to mortals eternal benefits.

Thousands upon thousands of heavenly spirits bless and adore you, myriads and myriads of angels, their spirits on fire, sing to your name. With the cherubim and seraphim, they glorify and adore your grandeur saying to each other as they proclaim unceasingly: Holy, Holy, Holy is the Lord of hosts; heaven and earth are filled with his wonderful presence, with the splendour of his greatness.

Hosanna in the highest, hosanna to the Son of David! Blessed is he who comes and who will come with heavenly power in the name of the Lord. Hosanna in the highest.

We affirm your presence, Lord, we, your servants, to whom you have made an immense gift which we cannot possibly repay.

You clothed yourself with our humanity, you came down from heaven with your divinity, you have raised up our littleness, lifted us from our prostration, raised to new life our mortal flesh, pardoned our sins, condoned our debt; you have brought light to our minds, vanquished our enemies, given honour to our poverty. Lord, our God may our song meetly give glory, acknowledgement and adoration to your superabundant grace, now and for ever and through all ages. Amen.

Chaldean liturgy

18

Initial O. David and Christ.

Prayer for the Nativity

esus Christ, radiant centre of glory,
image of our God, the invisible Father,
revealer of his eternal designs,
prince of peace;
father of the world to come . . .
For our sake he took the likeness of a slave,
becoming flesh in the womb of the Virgin Mary,
without intervention of man;
for our sake, wrapped in swaddling bands
and laid in a manger
adored by the shepherds
and hymned by the angelic powers, who sang:

> Glory to God in the heavens
> and on earth peace and good to men.

Make us worthy, Lord, to celebrate and to conclude in peace the
feast which magnifies the rising of your light,
by avoiding empty words, working with justice, fleeing from the
passions and raising up the spirit above earthly goods.
Bless your Church, formed long ago
to be united with yourself through your life-giving blood.
Come to the aid of your faithful shepherds,
of the priests and the teachers of your Gospel.
Bless your faithful whose only hope is in your mercy; christian souls,
the sick, those who are tormented in spirit and those who have
asked us to pray for them.
Have pity, in your infinite clemency, and preserve us in fitness to
receive the future, endless good things.
We celebrate your glorious nativity
with the Father who sent you for our redemption,
with the life-giving Spirit,
now and for ever and through all ages. Amen.

Syriac liturgy

The flight into Egypt
and the slaughter of the innocents at Bethlehem.

Prayer to the Divine Master

e propitious, O Father, Master, to your disciples;
O Father, Guide of Israel, Father and Son who are one:
Lord.
Grant to those who obey your precepts,
to be modelled in your image, and to enjoy,
after they have been proved, the goodness of God
and not the severity of his judgement.
Grant that we may all live in your peace,
that we may walk in the ways that lead to your city,
resolutely passing over the waters of sin,
sure of the guidance of the Holy Spirit,
your ineffable wisdom.
Grant that day and night, till our last hour,
we may pray in thanksgiving and give thanks in prayer
to the one Father and Son, the Son and the Father;
the Son, the leader and master,
together with the Holy Spirit.
All belongs to the One, in whom is all.
Through him all is one; eternity is his.
We are all his members; all ages are his glory.
To Goodness, to Beauty, to Wisdom,
To the Just One, all. To him be glory,
now and for all ages.
Amen.

Clement of Alexandria

*Triumphal entry of Jesus into Jerusalem
and the Last Supper with the apostles.*

Easter Hymn

 t is the Pasch; the Pasch of the Lord . . .
O you, who are truly all in all! . . .
The joy, the honour, the food and the delight of every
    creature;
through you the shadows of death have fled away,
and life is given to all,
the gates of heaven are flung open.
God becomes man
and man is raised up to the likeness of God.

O divine Pasch! . . .
O Pasch, light of new splendour . . .
The lamps of our souls will no more burn out.
The flame of grace,
divine and spiritual,
burns in the body and soul,
nourished by the resurrection of Christ.

We beg you, O Christ, Lord God,
eternal king of the spiritual world,
stretch out your protecting hands
over your holy Church
and over your holy people;
defend them, keep them, preserve them . . .

Raise up your standard over us
and grant that we may sing with Moses
the song of victory,
for yours is the glory and the power for all eternity!
Amen.

Hippolytus of Rome

24

Initial C (Cantate Domino). Inspired hagiographers.

A plea for pardon

esus, come, make yourself a servant for me.
Pour the water into the basin; come, wash my feet.
I know that what I ask is temerarious, but I fear your words:
"If I do not wash your feet, you can have no part with me".
Wash, then, my feet, that I may have a part with you.
But what do I say, wash my feet?
Peter could say this
for he needed only his feet to be washed
for he was all adamant.
But I, once bathed,
have need of that baptism
of which the Lord said:
"As for me, there is another baptism with which I must be baptised".

Origen

Mary, between Simeon and Anna, presents Jesus in the Temple.
The baptism of Jesus.

Prayer over the people

he hand of the only Son, alive and uncontaminated,
the hand which cures all our ills,
which sanctifies and protects,
is stretched out over the bowed heads of these people.
May the light of the Spirit,
the blessing of heaven,
the invocation of prophets and apostles
descend upon them.
May it keep their bodies pure in chastity,
their minds intent on study and the knowledge of the mystery.
All in union, may they be blessed
through your only Son, Jesus Christ;
through him your glory and omnipotence is known
in the Holy Spirit,
now and for all ages.
Amen.

Serapion of Thmuis

Second temptation of Jesus (he is carried by the devil
to the pinnacle of the Temple in Jerusalem).
Jesus raises to life the son of the widow of Nain.

Baptismal liturgy

 beg you, Son of the living God;
you have worked so many miracles;
you changed water into wine at Cana
to enlighten Israel;
you healed the eyes of the blind,
you restored hearing to deaf ears
and movement to paralysed limbs,
you corrected the stammering tongue,
freed the possessed,
made the lame run like the deer,
raised up the dead,
and taking him by the hand you made Peter
walk upon the water, safe from sinking.

You have left us this saying:
"Ask and you will receive,
knock and it will be opened to you.
All that you ask of the Father, in my name,
I too will ask of my Father, that you may have it".
I ask that I may receive, seek that I may find,
knock that it may be opened to me.
I ask in your name that you will ask your Father and
    he will hear me.
I am ready to pour out my blood,
as a victim, for your name's sake,
to bear any torment.
You, Lord, are the one who hears and protects me;
defend me from the enemy.
May the angel of light protect me,
for you have said, "What you ask of me
with faith in prayer, I will grant" . . .

Initial O. From Matthew 12, 35:
The good man brings good things out of his good treasure.

May your Spirit work in me; your will be accomplished in me,
that I may be wholly yours,
all the days of my life.

Attributed to Cyprian of Antioch

31

Communion chant

et us invoke Christ.
The sacred Body of Christ!
The lamb of God,
the sacred Body of him
who died for our salvation!

The sacred Body of him
who revealed the mystery of grace
of the new covenant
to his disciples.

The sacred Body which
washed with water
the feet of the apostles,
and with the Spirit
washed their souls.

The sacred Body which
pardoned the penitent woman;
the sacred Body whose blood
makes us clean.

The sacred body which
received the kiss of betrayal;
the sacred Body which
loved the world so much
as to accept even death on a cross.

We bless and glorify your name.

Fragment from an ancient eucharistic liturgy

Jesus Master between Elijah and Moses at the transfiguration.
First temptation to Jesus: to turn stones into bread.

Communion chant

 our sacrament, Lord Jesus Christ,
gives life
and the remission of sins;
you have suffered the passion for our sake.

For us you have drunk gall
to take from us all bitterness;

you have drunk a bitter wine for us
to lift us from our weariness;

you have been despised for us,
that the dew of immortality might be poured upon us;

you have been beaten with scourges
to ensure to our frailty eternal life;

you have been crowned with thorns
that your faithful might be crowned
    with the evergreen laurels of love;

you have been wrapped in a winding sheet
that we might be clothed in your strength;

you were laid in the tomb
that in a new age loving kindness might
    again be granted to us.

Fragment from an ancient eucharistic liturgy

Initial O. David and Christ.

Communion chant

he has given them a heavenly bread
and man has eaten the bread of angels.
He has given them a heavenly bread
we have received a bread of blessing:
the Body of Christ and his precious Blood.
The Lord . . . then took the bread,
and a saving drink, the chalice of life.
We have received the holy bread.
Let us bless the Lord who has done great things on all the earth.
All the people, praise the Lord,
exult with joy in the Lord, O you just:
you have received the Body and Blood of Christ.
We give you thanks, O Christ, our God,
because you have deigned to share with us
your Body and your Blood, O Saviour;
you have drawn to yourself our hearts . . .

Fragment from an ancient eucharistic liturgy

*Jesus washes the feet of his disciples
and is arrested in the garden of Gethsemane.*

Communion chant

ou, who once spoke to Moses
on mount Sinai,
have received from an immaculate Virgin
flesh that is free from all sin.

You who once pastured Israel,
now feed on the milk of a Mother
who has not known man.
O marvellous happening!

You who once punished kings
now save yourself from a king
by flight into Egypt.

You, seated in majesty [on a high throne]
were laid in a manger
retaining all your dignity.

And now, full of faith,
we praise the Mother and sing to the Son.

He who in heaven is God and has no mother,
has descended to earth and lived as though motherless.

To you be the glory!

Fragment from an ancient eucharistic liturgy

*Jesus being scourged in Pilate's praetorium
and dying on the cross between Mary and John.*

Canticle for the Easter vigil

oday we have contemplated upon the altar
our Lord Jesus Christ . . .
Today we have heard his voice, powerful yet gentle,
admonishing us:

This is the Body which burns up the thorns of sin
and gives light to the souls of men . . .
This is the Body in whose presence
the daughter of the Canaanite was cured.
This is the Body, which, approached
in full confidence by the sinful woman,
set her free from the mire of sin.
This is the Body Thomas touched
and recognising, cried out:
my Lord and my God.
This is the Body, great and most high,
which is the principle of our salvation.

One day he who is the Word
and our Life determined
that his blood should be poured out for us
and offered for the forgiveness of our sins.

We have drunk of the blood
by which we have been redeemed,
restored, instructed, given light.

Who is entitled to celebrate the mystery of grace?
we have been found worthy to share in this gift.
Let us keep it to the end that we may hear
from his holy and blessed voice:

"Come, O blessed, to my Father,
Receive the inheritance of the kingdom prepared for you".

Then those who crucified the Lord will fear;
those who have not believed in the Father, Son,
and Holy Spirit will be ashamed;
those who have denied and not borne witness to
the most holy Trinity, one God, will be lost.

As for us, beloved,
we celebrate the wonder of the baptism of Jesus,
his holy and life-giving resurrection,
through which salvation has come to the world.
We await the happy fulfilment of redemption
in the grace and love
of our Lord Jesus Christ,
to whom is due all glory, honour and adoration.

Fragment from an ancient eucharistic liturgy

Initial O. Jesus derisively crowned king.

Hymn for the Nativity

 ons of men,
　　do you truly speak of justice?
　　Dwellers on the earth,
　　do you truly judge with fairness?

We confess with unshakable faith
　　　that God, who was made man
　　　and who was given birth by a Virgin.

Before all time he was begotten
　　of an immeasurable Father;
　　　　now we adore him who became incarnate
　　　　in a Virgin's womb.

He is the creator of all,
　　　himself remaining invisible and distinct from creation.
So we are able to say:
　　　in you, Lord, is clemency; glory be to you.

O holy God,
　　　you have deigned to be born, a tiny child, from a Virgin.
O God, holy and strong,
　　　you have willed to rest in the arms of Mary.
O God, holy and immortal,
　　　you have come to rescue Adam from hell.

O immaculate Virgin, Mother of God, full of grace,
　　　Emmanuel, whom you have carried,
　　　is the fruit of your womb.
In your maternal bosom you have nourished all men.
You are above all praise and all glory.
Hail, Mother of God, joy of the angels.

The fullness of your grace
　　　goes beyond what the prophets foretold.
The Lord is with you,
　　　you have given birth
　　　to the Saviour of the world.

Fragment from an ancient eucharistic liturgy

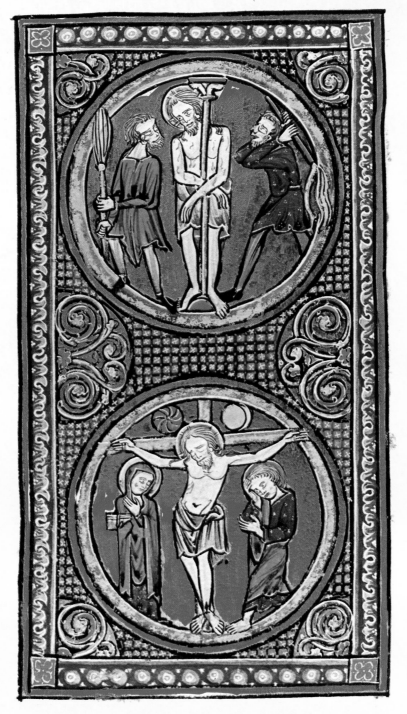

Jesus, at supper with Simon the leper at Bethany,
pardons and defends the woman caught in adultery.

Easter hymn

e glorify you, O Christ, singing: glory to the Lord!
He was born of the Holy Spirit in order to give us life.
He deigned to dwell among us.
To him we render our veneration,
crying out together: glory to the Lord!

Behold: the Virgin has given birth to Emmanuel.
He has come down from heaven,
has saved from Egypt a people that was lost.
Let us exalt him, crying: glory to the Lord!

He has willed to overcome our enemy;
has made his dwelling in the Virgin Mary:
the invisible has become visible in flesh.
Let us adore hm, crying out: glory to the Lord!

Born of a woman ever virgin,
the Word of truth rose again for us.
Let us celebrate the Lord,
intoning: glory to the Lord!

Light from light, Christ our king
is risen for us.
He has saved us from the land of Egypt;
all together let us sing: glory to the Lord!

Fragment from an ancient eucharistic liturgy

44

Initial E. A musician ringing bells by percussion.

To Christ the first-born

 he stars that shine and the powers in motion
all vanish in the splendour of your light
and remain still before the power of your greatness.
You alone are visible,
you reveal the image of the Father almighty,
and thus you manifest the sublimity of the Father and the Son.
As the Father is almighty in the heavenly sphere,
so are you, the Son, in our universe
the first-born, the guide and lord of all power;
you, from the beginning, are the second grandeur
that comes from that of the Father;
you are the foundation of all the world.
You are our archetype,
the mind which ordains and the one who steers;
you are the way and the door that opens into light.
You are the image of justice;
you are ever our shining star.
To you we render thanks, praise and blessing.
Before you we bend the knee
and we ask, with trust, that we be made holy.
Grant that we may be ever strong in faith,
sound in mind and body
to sing for ever and without ceasing your praises,
that you, the Immortal, the Infinite, the Eternal
may be celebrated in every place.
You are the model and essence of the Spirit,
you are our blessed Father,
our king and our God.
With eyes fixed on you, we shall not die, O Lord;
if we confess your name we shall not be lost.

Anonymous hymn

Initial B (Beatus vir qui non ambulat in via impiorum).
David the psalmist and crowned king.

Evening hymn

O Christ Jesus, radiant light
of the immortal glory of the Father of heaven!
As the sun sinks to its setting
we are face to face with the twilight of evening:
we honour God, Father, Son and Holy Spirit.
You are worthy ever to be hymned by voices that are pure,
Son of God who gives us life.
The universe proclaims your glory.

Primitive liturgy

Initial O. The crucified Jesus with the Father enthroned.

Prayer to Christ

e who is immortal
has suffered much for us.
Come to help us, Son of God, born of Mary!
Christ Jesus, come to our aid, born of Mary!

Heavenly shoot from the stock of David,
come to our aid, O Son, born of Mary!
Christ Jesus, come to our aid, O Son, born of Mary!

May the immortal Son be praised over all the earth.
Come to our aid, O Son, born of Mary!
Christ Jesus, come to our aid, O Son, born of Mary!

In your clemency, you came from heaven to earth.
Come to our aid, O Son, born of Mary!
Christ Jesus, come to our aid, O Son, born of Mary!

Master of true life from all eternity.
Come to our aid, O Son, born of Mary!
Christ Jesus, come to our aid, O Son, born of Mary!

Egyptian epigraph

Jesus taken down from the cross.
The descent into hell.

Prayer from the anaphora of Gregory

O Christ, our God, we beg you:
give stability and strength to the Church,
implant in the depths of our souls
the harmony of love,
that the integrity of faith may grow.
Give firmness to the shepherds
and soundness to the flock.
May the clergy be irreprehensible in their morals,
the monks continent,
the virgins pure,
married couples in accord;
may the penitent receive your pardon;
the rich be generous,
those in power, moderate;
may the poor receive help.
Be strength to the old
and teacher to the young.
Enlighten those without faith,
make divisions in the Church to cease,
break the pride of heretics
and deign to hold all united
in concord and love.

Coptic liturgy

Jesus laid in the sepulchre of Joseph of Arimathea,
and rising again on the third day.

Prayer before martyrdom

ord, God almighty, Jesus Christ, who came to call not the just but sinners to repentance, in fulfilment of your promise you have graciously said: In the moment that the sinner repents of his fault, I forget his sin.

Accept my repentance in this hour of pain, and by means of this fire prepared for my body, set me free from the eternal fire that would burn both soul and body.

I thank you, Lord Jesus Christ, for having accepted me as a holocaust to your name. I thank you for having offered yourself on the cross as a victim for the whole world; you, the just for the unjust; the good for the evil; you, the innocent, a victim for sinners.

I offer my sacrifice to you, who with the Father and the holy Spirit, live and reign, God, for ever and ever. Amen!

Afra of Augusta

The angel shows the empty tomb to the women.
Mary Magdalen and the Risen Jesus.

Hymn for Ascension Day

O n this day the new bread of the spirit
has gone up to heaven.
The mysteries were revealed in your Body
which has gone up as an offering.
Blessed be your bread, O Lord!

The Lamb has come to us from the house of David;
the priest, from the stock of Abraham,
has become for our sakes the Lamb of God,
the new minister of sacrifice.

His body is the victim, his blood is our drink.
Blessed be the new sacrifice!

He has descended from heaven like the light;
is born of Mary as a divine shoot;
as a fruit he has fallen from the cross;
and is offered up to heaven as the first fruits.
Blessed be his will!

You are the offering of heaven and of earth,
immolated and at the same time adored.
You came to be a victim,
you ascended as a singular offering,
you ascended, Lord,
bearing with you the offering of your sacrifice.

Ephrem Syrus

Jesus ascending into heaven.
The descent of the Holy Spirit on the apostles in the cenacle.

Prayer of an old man

Lord, Christ Jesus, king of kings, you have power over life and death; you know the intimate secrets and none of our thoughts and sentiments are unknown to you. Repair the evil which I have done in your sight.

My life declines from day to day and my sin is growing. O Lord, God of soul and body, you know the extreme frailty of my soul and of my flesh, give strength to my weakness and sustain me in my anguish.

You, who are my powerful support, know that I am esteemed by many. Give me a grateful heart, which will not forget your benefits, Lord of infinite goodness! Forget my many sins and pardon all my treachery.

Lord, do not despise the prayer of one who is sorry; keep me in your grace as you have kept me in the past. This has shown me the wisdom of: blessed are those who pass swiftly through life, for they will receive a crown of glory.

Lord, I praise and glorify you in spite of my unworthiness, for your mercy to me has been without limit. You are my help and my protector. May your name be ever praised!

To you, O Lord our God, be glory!

Ephrem Syrus

Initial B
(Benedicta sit sancta Trinitas).
Jesus Master and two disciples.

Prayer to the suffering Christ

I fall in adoration at your feet, Lord!
I thank you, God of goodness;
God of holiness, I invoke you,
on my knees, in your sight . . .

For me, an unworthy sinner,
you have willed to undergo the death of the cross,
setting me free from the bonds of evil.

What shall I offer you in return for your generosity?

Glory to you, friend of men!
Glory to you, most merciful!
Glory to you, most patient!
Glory to you who forgive sin!
Glory to you who have come to save us!
Glory to you who have been made man in the womb of a Virgin!
Glory to you who have been bound!
Glory to you who have been scourged!
Glory to you who have been derided!
Glory to you who have been nailed to the cross!
Glory to you, laid in the sepulchre, but risen again!
Glory to you who have preached the Gospel to men
    and have been believed!
Glory to you who have ascended to heaven!
Glory to you, seated at the right hand of the Father
    and who will return with him, in majesty, among the angels,
    to judge those who have disregarded your passion!

The powers of heaven will be shaken;
all the angels and archangels, the cherubim and seraphim
will appear in fear and trembling before your glory;
the foundations of the earth will quake
and all that has life will cry out before your majesty.

In that hour let your hand draw me beneath your wings,
and save me from the terrible fire, from the gnashing of teeth,
from the outer darkness and from despair without end.
That I may sing to your glory:
glory to him who through his merciful goodness
has designed to redeem the sinner.

Ephrem Syrus

Initial G (Gaudeamus omnes in Domino).
Jesus derisively crowned with thorns by the soldiers
in Pilate's praetorium.

Paschal doxology

O Pasch, great and holy mystery that purifies the universe,
I would speak to you as if you had a soul.
O Word of God, light and life, wisdom and power!
I greet you with your many names.
Illustrious shoot, breath and image of the Spirit!
O Word of God, visible being in whom all is assumed
and all governed by your power!
Deign to listen to my words:
they are not the beginning
but certainly the fulfilment of my offering.
Grant that they may be both thanksgiving and supplication.
Grant that I may bear only the trials of the spirit
that bring the reward assigned to our life.
Lighten the weight of the body;
You know, O Lord, how heavily it weighs.
Mitigate the severity of your judgment,
when we come to be winnowed by you.
But if our desires will be realised
grant that we may set out on our way and find welcome
in the heavenly mansions.
We will go on offering to you an acceptable sacrifice,
on your altar, Father, Word and Holy Spirit.
To you be the glory, the honour and the power through all ages.
Amen.

Gregory Nazianzen

Initial I (Introduxit vos Dominus in terram).
Jesus and the two disciples on the way
and at table together at Emmaus.

Hymn for the night

O Christ, Word of God,
light of light, without beginning,
help of the Spirit, we praise you.
Threefold light of one undivided glory,
we praise you.

You have banished the darkness and created the light
and in this you have created all things.
To matter you have given life
giving it the imprint of the face of the world
and the traits of its beauty.

You have illumined man's spirit
with reason and wisdom.
Your eternal light is reflected everywhere,
so that, in the light, man might discover
true beauty, and all become luminous.

You have lit up the heavens with variegated lights.
The night and the day you have commanded to take turns
in a rule of fraternal friendship;
the first brings to an end the fatigue of the body,
the other spurs us on to work as commanded;
and we flee from the darkness
to hasten towards that day
which no sadness of the night
can ever bring to an end.

Give to my eyelids a light slumber
that my voice may not long remain silent.
While created things watch to sing psalms with the angels,
may my sleep be ever restful in your presence;
may the night make me oblivious of the day's sins,
and its oddities not beset my dreams.

Even if my body is inert
my spirit, O God, gives you praise!
Father, Son and Holy Spirit,
to you be honour and glory and power
through all ages. Amen.

Gregory Nazianzen

Initial M
(Me expectaverunt peccatores).
St Agnes with two other saints.
She carries the book of the Scriptures
while a lamb lies at her feet.
The saint being carried up to heaven.

Prayer in sickness

ive me strength, O Christ. Your servant is undone.
My voice, singing to you, is now silent.
How can you allow it?
Give me strength, and do not abandon your minister.
I would have health once more;
sing to your praise and sanctify your people.
I beg you, my strength, do not desert me.
If my faith has grown less in the storm,
yet I would return to you.

Gregory Nazianzen

Initial V (Viri Galilei quid admiramini).
Jesus ascending into heaven. Mary with the apostles.

To the eternal creator of the world

ternal maker of the world,
who rules over night and day
dividing up our daily round
to ease the body's weariness.

O night light for wayfarers
Which distinguishes night from night,
the dawn bird now sings aloud
calling up the light of the sun.

Lucifer [day star], unveiled by him,
drives darkness from the face of heaven
and malefactors in their troops
abandon now their brigandage.

Sailors gain strength as he appears,
and the sea's waves grow calm again;
hearing him, the Rock of the Church
[Peter] weeping, mourns his sin.

Let us arise then speedily.
The cock awakens those who sleep
and rouses up the drowsy ones;
the perjurors are accused by him.

At cock crow hope is born again,
and health returns to those who ail;
the brigand hides his dagger now,
and faith revives in apostate soul.

Jesus, look on those who waver;
and, looking, help us to be firm;
under your care shame fades away
and tears wipe out the stain of sin.

O light, shine now within our souls
and torpor fly from every mind;
and at the dawn our voices rise
in songs of prayer and praise to you.

Ambrose

Initial G (Gaudeamus omnes in Domino).
Jesus in glory among angels and saints
(perfect balance of three men and three women saints.)

Easter hymn

O night clearer than the day!
O night more luminous than the sun!
O night whiter than the snow!
giving more light than our torches,
sweeter than Paradise!
O night that knows no darkness;
driving away our sleep,
you make us keep watch with the angels.
O night, the terror of the demons,
paschal night, awaited for a year!
The Church's wedding night
which gives life to the newly baptised
and renders harmless the torpidity of the demon.
Night in which the Heir
brings the heirs into eternity.

Asterius of Amasea

70

Initial G (Gaudeamus omnes in Domino).
The Risen Jesus and Mary Magdalen.

Hymn to Christ the light and life

O Christ come among men
as source of light,
your ineffable birth
is before the beginning of time.
You are the radiant light shining with the Father.
You irradiate lustreless matter
and illumine the souls of the faithful.

You have created the world
and fixed the orbit of the stars;
you sustain the axis of the earth,
you save all mankind.
You guide the sun in its course
to light up all our days
and the crescent moon
which dispels the darkness of night.
You make the seed to sprout
preparing food for the flocks.
From your inexhaustible fount
you pour out the splendour of life
making fruitful the whole universe . . .

Synesius of Cyrene

Initial I (Invoca me et ego exaudiam).
Jesus and two angels. Satan, the tempter, is under
the aspect of a vile animal with horns and vomiting flames.

Evening hymn

ive to us, O Lord, the peace of the evening
and save us from the snares of the enemy
in the strength of your holy and victorious
cross.
Lord of my salvation,
I implore you day and night,
may my prayers come unto you,
bend your ear to my pleading.
May there come to us, O Lord,
a guardian sent by you
to protect us always.
Implant in us, O Lord,
the power of your holy cross
which will protect us always.
Make us worthy, O Lord,
to spend this evening
in peace and without temptation.
Deign, O Lord,
during this night,
to keep us in peace and without sin.
The Lord God is with us;
know this, you nations, and be bewildered;
for God is with us.
In him will we hope
and he will be our salvation;
because God is with us . . .
And the people that dwelt in darkness
see the great light;
for God is with us.
And you who live in darkness
and in the shadow of death,
light will shine upon you;
because God is with us.

And we have been given a Son;
    for God is with us.
And the dominion
will be on his shoulders;
because God is with us.
    And his name will be
    "Messenger of the great mystery";
    for God is with us.
And "Wonderful Counsellor";
because God is with us.
    And "God the strong prince";
    because God is with us.
And the "Prince of peace",
"Father of the world to come";
the "Lord God with us".

Armenian liturgy

Initial I (In medio Ecclesiae aperuit os).
The story of St John the evangelist in a series
of seven pictures.

In praise of the Cross

O Cross, ineffable love of God and glory of heaven!
Cross, eternal salvation; Cross, terror of the reprobate.
O Cross, support of the just, light of Christians,
for you, God became a slave in the flesh, here on earth;
by your means, man in God is crowned king in heaven;
from you streams the true light, victorious over accursed night.
You gave believers power to make
the pantheon of the nations quake;
you are the soul of peace
that unites men in Christ the mediator;
you are the ladder for man to climb to heaven.
Be always for us, your faithful, both pillar and anchor;
watch over our homes, set the course of our ship.
In the Cross may our faith remain strong,
and there be our crown prepared.

Paulinus of Nola

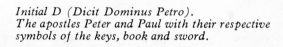

Initial D (Dicit Dominus Petro).
The apostles Peter and Paul with their respective
symbols of the keys, book and sword.

Morning hymn

festive chirrupping announces the day,
singing in the light of dawn.
Christ spurs on the soul,
inviting us to a rebirth, this day.

Arise from your beds, he urges,
where a feeble languor makes you inert.
Be watchful, chaste, good, and sober;
for I am close to you.

Let us invoke Jesus, aloud,
sorrowing, praying, repentant;
an ardent invocation
keeps a pure heart on the alert.

O Christ, drive away sleep,
break the chains of night,
make good the ancient fault,
bring to us new light.

Glory be to God the Father,
and to his only Son,
together with the Spirit, the consoler,
now and for ever.

Prudentius

Initial R
(Resurrexi et adhuc tecum sum).
The three Marys at the empty tomb
with the angel
and meeting the Risen Jesus.

Preface for Epiphany

O n the banks of the Jordan
[Father] your voice resounded
in the roll of thunder coming from heaven
making manifest the Saviour,
showing yourself as Father of eternal light.
You have rent the heavens,
blessed the air,
purified the water,
made manifest your only Son
through the Holy Spirit
appearing in the form of a dove.
Today the fountains, having received your blessing,
cast off the ancient curse;
and so, the faithful, purified from their sins,
are presented to God, for eternal life,
as sons by adoption.
In fact those who through birth in the flesh
were destined for the life of time,
those whom death had seized through the complicity of sin
are welcomed into eternal life
and brought back to the glory of heaven.

Ambrosian liturgy

Initial H (Hodie in Iordane baptizato Domino).
The Magi adoring Jesus in the arms of Mary
at Bethlehem.

Preface for Easter

I t is necessary, and for our well-being, to give you thanks
God, holy and almighty,
   to celebrate your praise with devotion, Father of glory,
   creator and author of the universe,
through your Son, Jesus Christ.
He, being God, full of majesty, humbled himself
to the point of accepting the punishment of the cross
for the salvation of men.
In the depth of ages
Abraham prefigured this in his son;
the people of Moses with the paschal lamb they immolated.
He it is of whom
announcement was made by the voice of the prophets:
he would take upon himself the sins of all men,
cancel out the whole of our misdeeds.
This is the great Pasch
which the blood of Christ has covered with glory,
making the Christian people exult with joyous devotion!
O mystery of grace!
Inexpressible mystery of divine munificence!
O festival most venerated among all festivals,
in which he abandoned himself to men
even unto death, to save mere slaves!
O blessed death, which has broken the chains of death!
Now the prince of hell is vanquished,
and we, saved from the abyss of guilt,
exult in joy and take with Christ once more
the road to heaven.

Ambrosian liturgy

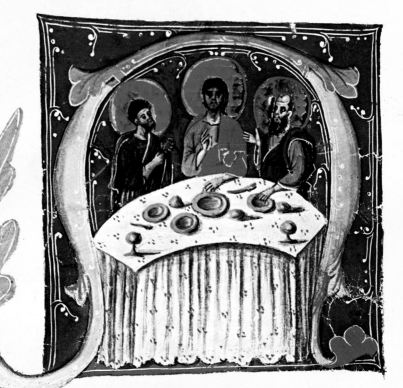

Initial M
(Miti autem nimis honorati sunt amici).
Jesus at table with the disciples
at Emmaus.

Canticle for the resurrection of Lazarus

ord of the heavens, merciful father of the humble,
who by a single word restored Lazarus to life,
grant to those who have gone before us
the grace to contemplate the light of your countenance.

Give us the grace to live in peace in our time,
to accept the death you have prepared for us,
to be guided, both in life
and in death, by your will.

Give but a sign, a word,
O Lord, and already we are saved.

You will not abandon those who love you
but keep them in life, and call them to yourself who are risen.
You are the resurrection and the life.

Romanos the Melodious

Initial N
(Nunc scio vere quia misit Dominus).
St Peter leaving the prison
with the angel who freed him
holding him by the hand.

Prayer for help

ave pity, O Christ,
on those who believe in you.
You are the God of glory
for all ages.

Hasten to the aid of those who suffer,
make speed to comfort those in trouble.

Father of believers, life of the living,
God who is over all, for there is no-one above you.

Creator of all things, universal judge,
Lord over princes, God of the world.

Sublime majesty of the heavenly Jerusalem,
king, glory, and triumph of the kingdom.

God of eternal light, inexpressible,
highest, most loveable, beyond compare.

Great and clement God, wise and omniscient,
mover of all things, ancient and new.

Pope Pelagius I

Initial D (Dominus secus mare Galileae).
Jesus calling the two fishermen
Peter and Andrew of Bethsaida
to be his disciples.

Hymn to the Cross

he regal banners now advance,
now shines the mystery of the cross
on which the Creator of mankind
made man, was raised on high to die.

With arms fast bound and nailed hands
the cross-piece fixed, we now behold
the sign of our redemption there
where Clemency the victim makes.

His side, sore wounded by the point,
transpiercing, of the cruel lance,
to cleanse the world from sinful stain
pours blood and water from the wound.

Now is the prophecy fulfilled
of David speaking with such truth
when to the nations he foretold
that God would reign upon a tree.

O shining and majestic tree
adorned with regal mantle now,
most noble trunk, chosen to bear
limbs of such great sanctity.

O blessed tree, that with your arms
support the Saviour of the world
a balance for that flesh divine
that snatched away the prey of hell.

From your bark a perfume breathes
in sweetness surpassing nectar far,
proudly you bear the fertile fruit
while shouts acclaim his triumph now.

From the glory of the Passion
praise to the altar and Victim blest
in passion, undergoing death,
with death, restoring life again.

Hail cross, our one and only hope,
in this our time of mourning, grant
that all the faithful grow in grace
and sinners have their guilt forgiven.

O Trinity, the source of life,
all spirits sing their praise to you.
To those time-bound give comfort still,
who by the cross have been redeemed.

Venantius Fortunatus

Initial A (Aspiciens a longe ecce video Dei potentiam).
Jesus Master in glory and nine prophets
with scrolls of the Scriptures.

Prayer to obtain forgiveness

ardon, Lord; pardon your people
whom you have redeemed with your blood, O Christ;
may your anger not weigh upon us.

We pray you for your infinite clemency;
turn away your wrath from this city
and turn from this holy house.

We have sinned against you
and you have been angry with us
and no one can flee from your punishments.

We have sinned against you, O Lord,
we have sinned.
Be merciful to us, set us free from ills
which every day fall upon us.

Pardon, O Lord, the sins of your people,
according to your infinite generosity.

You once showed kindness to our fathers:
be merciful to us and your glory
will shine out in our lives.

Pardon, O Lord, those who have sinned;
give your grace to those who repent;
have pity on us who pray to you,
O Christ, Saviour of the world.

Jesus, look upon us
and have pity. Amen.

Hibernian-Celtic hymnody

Initial C (Circumdederunt me gemitus).
Jesus Master and a boy with a hatchet on his shoulder.

Prayer for salvation

y Saviour, grant that the arduous task of my
salvation may be brought to a happy conclusion.
May neither the lashing rains,
   nor the impetus of torrents racing down from the
mountains,
nor the violent storm be able to shake my house.

With your victorious hand, assist me, Lord!
Be my help, preserve my life,
that I may praise you, the giver and Lord of all that is most precious
and the salvation of men.

Without you, Almighty, no work would exist,
no project, no idea, no proposal, no security,
nor any of those things that
would serve to attain the final end.

You have created and given me, both soul and body;
you have raised me up when I had fallen,
and have shown me the way to heaven.

And you will bring me in, without merit of mine,
to your house to live with you in eternity
and to sing a hymn to your glory
along with all the blessed.

Maximus

Initial Q (Quasi modo geniti infantes).
The apostle Thomas touching the wound in Christ's side.

Christmas prayer

 e praise you, Lord Jesus Christ,
God-Saviour of men,
stupendously powerful with the Father;
we praise you, we invoke you, we pray to you;
assist us with your pardon, with clemency give us your grace.

Awaken in our hearts desires deserving of fulfilment;
suggest to us words that are worthy to be heard;
grant that our actions may be worthy of blessing.

We beg you to renew your birth in human nature,
penetrating us with your invisible godhead
as you did in a unique way in Mary
and do now spiritually in the Church.

May you be conceived by our faith,
that a mind untouched by corruption may bring you forth,
that the soul, ever confirmed by the power of the Most High,
may offer you a dwelling place.

Be not born in us, but reveal yourself in us.
Be truly for us the Emmanuel, God with us.

Deign to remain with us, to fight for us.
Only so can we conquer.

Mozarabic liturgy

94

Initial H
(Hodie scietis quia veni).
Angels announcing from heaven
the good news
of the birth of Jesus
to three shepherds.

Lenten hymn

emain, O Christ, in the hearts you have redeemed.
You who are perfect love,
pour into our words
sincere repentance.

We raise our prayer to you,
O Jesus, with faith;
pardon the sin we have committed.

By the holy sign of the cross,
by your tortured body,
defend us constantly as your sons.

The Venerable Bede

Initial L
(*Laetemur omnes in Domino*).
Conversion of St Paul.
Saul, dressed as a warrior
with sword in hand,
in dialogue with an angel
who speaks to him from heaven.

Prayer for the catholic Church

e beg you, good Jesus, our Lord,
by the intercession of the glorious Virgin Mary
your Mother, and of all angels and saints,
to increase the faith of your catholic Church,
to grant us peace and forgive our sins.

Grant health to the sick,
a good journey and happy arrival
to those who travel by land or sea,
serenity to those who suffer,
liberty to the oppressed;
to slaves, to the vanquished, to pilgrims,
liberty, clemency and return to their homeland.

Send your holy angel on sentry
over those who place obstacles to fraternal charity;
in your kindness grant true faith to those who believe not,
and eternal repose to those of our brothers
who have died in the faith.

Alcuin's Liturgical Collection

Initial E (Etenim sederunt principes).
Martyrdom of St Stephen.
As the persecutors stone him Stephen beholds
Christ in glory.

Thanksgiving to Jesus

ord Jesus, I give you thanks,
not only with the lips and heart,
which often comes to little, but with the spirit,
with which I speak to you, question you,
love you, and recognise you.
You are my all, and everything is in you.
In you we live, and move, and have our being.

You are our father, our brother, our all;
and to those who love you, you have promised such things
as no one has ever seen or thought of,
no one ever enjoyed.

Make the gift of these things to your humble faithful;
you who are God, true and good,
and there is no other besides you.

You are the true God, the true Son of God,
to whom be honour and glory and majesty
in eternity and for all ages to come.

Gallican Formularies

100

Initial A (Ad te levavi animam meam).
Jesus Master in glory among angels and saints.

Ode to Christ the saviour

hrist incarnate makes me worthy of God,
Christ humbled for me, raises me high,
Christ, the giver of life,
suffering in human nature,
makes me impassive.
And so, I sing a hymn of thanksgiving,
to him who is glorified.

Christ crucified raises me high,
Christ who is slain makes me rise again with him;
Christ gives me life.
And so, clapping my hands with joy,
I sing to the saviour a hymn of victory,
to him who is glorified.

Cosmas of Maiuma

Initial I (Iudica me Deus).
Jesus and the Pharisees.
He is disputing with four of them above
and six below.

Ode to Christ crucified

y the tree of the cross
you have healed the bitterness of the tree,
and have opened Paradise to men.
Glory be to you, Lord!

Now we are no longer prevented
from coming to the tree of life;
we have hope in your cross.
Glory be to you, Lord!

O Immortal One, nailed to the wood,
you have triumphed over the snares of the devil.
Glory be to you, Lord!

You, who for my sake have submitted
to being placed on the cross,
accept my vigilant celebration of praise,
O Christ, God, Friend of men.

Lord of the heavenly armies,
who knows my carelessness of soul,
save me by your cross,
O Christ, God, Friend of men.

Brighter than fire, more luminous than flame,
have you shown the wood of your cross, O Christ.
Burn away the sins of the sick and enlighten the hearts
of those who, with hymns, celebrate
your voluntary crucifixion.
Christ, God, glory to you!

Christ, God,
who for us accepted a sorrowful crucifixion,
accept all who sing hymns to your passion,
and save us.

Byzantine liturgy

104

*Initial D (Dominus ne longe facias auxilium).
Jesus, in agony in the garden of Gethsemane,
is comforted by an angel while the three
chosen disciples sleep.*

Plea for protection

ith the seal of the cross,
impressed with your blood,
with which we have been baptized
to make us ready for adoption,
you have modelled us into the image of your glory.
By all these divine gifts,
Satan be put to confusion, his plots overturned,
his snares evaded, the enemy vanquished,
his sharp weapons repelled,
light shine through the gloom,
darkness be dispelled,
mists fade away.
Would that your arms might receive us
into your protection,
your right hand press its seal upon us.
You are indeed full of love and clemency
and your name is invoked over your faithful.
To you, together with the Father,
through the Holy Spirit,
be glory and majesty through all ages. Amen.

Gregory of Narek

Initial L (Loquebar de testimoniis).
St Catherine, virgin and martyr.
Her martyrdom (bottom);
being taken to Sinai by two angels (centre);
with Christ in glory (top).

Prayer to Christ the creator

 Sun of justice, blessed ray,
the first source of light;
O ardently Desired, above all else;
powerful, inscrutable, ineffable;
joy of the good, vision of fulfilled hope,
praised and heavenly, Christ the Creator;
king of glory, assurance of life,
fill the void of my miserable voice
with your almighty word;
and offer it as a supplication
pleasing to your Father Most High,
for you have come into the world in likeness to me,
subjecting yourself to human suffering,
the heritage of the curse.
O blessing of life, watchful providence
for all, both small and great!
If you accepted to die for me,
you, God and Lord of all,
how much more,
for the sake of the body you assumed, of your nature,
will you pardon the weakness that leads me into danger,
interceding for me, a sinner,
with the Father whose glory you share.

Gregory of Narek

Initial S (Scio cui credidi).
Martyrdom of St Paul.

INDEX

Sources

The first Christian prayer. Gospel according to Luke (11, 2-4). *Page 10.*

The Gospels contain two versions of the prayer taught by Jesus, that of Matthew (6, 9-13) and that of Luke (11, 2-4). Matthew's text, adopted by the Liturgy, is certainly closer to the Aramaic and Hebrew original; Luke's is all of a piece with his Gospel, written for the Gentiles (the people outside the Hebrew world, the pagans) and so some things that might seem too Semitic in character, such as the expression "who art in heaven" and the word "debt" which has been changed to "sin" (the Jews regarded sin as a debt due to God), have been omitted; it reveals, however, his preoccupation to search out the maximum clarity of thought. The brief formula appears to take into account Jesus' invitation to pray as he himself teaches; even to pray in secret, as in recollection everyone has the possibility to make his own aspirations. And so it seems fitting to open this volume with the prayer taught by Jesus as it is preserved for us by Luke.

Invocations before martyrdom. Ignatius of Antioch. *Page 12.*

Ignatius, bishop of Antioch, called "Theophorus" (God-bearer), was taken to Rome and thrown to the wild beasts in the circus during the Trajan persecution (98-117). The persecution years are the only means we have for dating Ignatius. He was the first in importance among the Apostolic Fathers. He was a man of vigorous talent, animated by a lively faith in God and a mystic ardour. On his way to Rome, in chains, he wrote seven magnificent letters, anxious to guard the faithful against heresy and exhort them to maintain union with their bishop. Most notable, in fact, incomparable, is the Letter to the Romans from which we take this invocation pronounced by Ignatius when faced with the certainty of martyrdom. *Patrologia Graeca 5, 692.*

Prayer at the stake. Polycarp of Smyrna. *Page 14.*

Polycarp (c. 70-c. 156), bishop of Smyrna, friend of Ignatius and teacher of Irenaeus of Lyons, was a disciple of the Apostle John. He was burnt to death as a martyr about the year 156, under the Emperor Antoninus Pius. The account of his martyrdom was set down shortly after his death by a certain Marcion, and is considered worthy of belief. They tied him to the stake. Tied thus, with his hands behind his back, Polycarp looked like a lamb chosen from the flock to be sacrificed. As the flames surrounded him, the martyr pronounced the following prayer; a solemn prayer, nourished by the scriptures, in which we can already hear the accents of the great doxology of the *Gloria. Patrologia Graeca 5, 1040.*

Prayer to Christ. Acts of Peter. *Page 16.*

The Acts of Peter, a small book extant only in a mutilated form, was written by an unknown author between 180 and 190, in Syria or Palestine. It belongs, like the apocryphal gospels, to that vast literature imitating the New Testament, which abounded in the first centuries and which did not find a place among those the Church recognised to be inspired books.

The apocryphal texts, in fact, while containing a nucleus of historical material, have the tone of popular narrative, giving rein to fantasy in order to satisfy curiosity concerning particulars on which the sacred narrative maintains silence, and favouring dreams and visions such as were dear to a primitive community. The Acts of Peter were translated into various languages; the incomplete Latin version is contained in the Acts of Vercelli, where the celebrated episode of Peter and Simon Magus is narrated. Text in L. Vouaux, *Les Actes de Pierre*, Paris 1922, p. 116.

Offertory Prayer. Chaldean liturgy. *Page 18.*

The anaphora, or prayer or the moment of the offertory, from the Chaldean liturgy is apparently very ancient — contemporary with that of Hippolytus of Rome (3rd century). Its provenance would seem to be Edessa (Northern Mesopotamia; today the Turkish city of Urfi) from where it passed into Syria. It is still in use by the Nestorians, the Christians of Malabar (India) and the Uniate Chaldean rite. The anaphora has been critically studied and published by B. Botte, *L'Anaphore Chaldeenne des Apotres*, in "Orientalia Christiana Periodica", XV, pp. 259-276.

Prayer for the Nativity. Syriac liturgy. *Page 20.*

It is difficult to give any date to the Syriac prayer reproduced here, but it reveals the characteristics of a very ancient form along with sobriety on the titles given to the Virgin Mary. Christ the Saviour is invoked on the day of the nativity on behalf of the many needs of his people and in a broad vision of charity imploring present well-being and the future Good for one's neighbour. Its content and elegant style make it a prototype for the prayer of the faithful. Text in *Oriens Christianus*, 1941, pp. 60-65.

Prayer to the Divine Master. Clement of Alexandria. *Page 22.*

Clement of Alexandria was a great thinker who, by his work as teacher (Origen was among his disciples) and by his writings, had a decisive and even audacious influence on Christian literature, so much so that he is considered the founder of "theological science". Among his principal works, of an apologetic and pastoral character, is *The Pedagogue* which develops a pedagogy and Christian ethic through the following of Christ, the master of life, and docile attention to Christ's teaching. The magnificent hymn to Christ, the last end and the norm of all things, from which we give an extract, closes the work. *Patrologia Graeca* 8, 680-684.

Easter hymn. Hippolytus of Rome. *Page 24.*

Hippolytus of Rome, more likely Greek by birth, is famous as an exegete and writer, and as a pugnatious opponent of heresy. But the style he adopted as a polemicist turned him into a libellist. On account of disciplinary questions he is reckoned as the first anti-pope. During the persecution of Maximus (235-238) he was condemned to hard labour in the mines of Sardinia, along with Pope Pontianus. He was reconciled and died a martyr with him in 235 or 236. In addition to the *Apostolic Tradition,* one of the earliest examples of liturgical ritual, Hippolytus wrote exegetical, dogmatic and disciplinary tracts. His tract on the Pasch is certainly the inspiration for this hymn for Easter, which seems to belong to a much later epoch; some scholars, however, attribute it to Hippolytus. The text is to be found in *Homily VI on the Pasch* (among homilies falsely attributed to John Chrysostom). *Patrologia Graeca* 59, 741-746. We give chosen passages.

A plea for pardon. Origen. *Page 26.*

Origen (Alexandria in Egypt 185-Tyre 253 or 254) is regarded as the greatest theologian of the Greek Church. His father Leonidas suffered martyrdom in the persecution of Septimius Severus (193-211) and Origen himself, in his old age, was tortured under Decius (249-251) but allowed to go free. Origen, by his intelligence, profound faith, mystical enthusiasm and culture, dominated the ecclesiastical, theological, apologetical, biblical and ascetic science of his time and is the greatest ecclesiastical writer of the epoch preceding Augustine. In him was united profane culture with a singular knowledge of scripture which he studied as textual critic and commentator, searching out the allegorical and spiritual meaning. Some of his homilies commenting on scripture end with an invocation, a turning to Christ, which is marked by a strongly personal note of affective piety. We give here the prayer for pardon which ends the *Fifth Homily on Isaiah. Patrologia Graeca* 13, 235-236.

Prayer over the people. Serapion of Thmuis. *Page 28.*

At the end of last century, an important collection of prayers (Euchology) was found on Mount Athos. Two of these bear the name of Serapion who was abbot of the monastery of Thmuis in Lower Egypt from the year 339, and a friend of Athanasius. It has not been critically proved that the other prayers of the Euchology, thirty in all, are by the same Serapion. The Euchology represents a primitive liturgical collection of ancient Egypt and includes the prayer for the eucharistic celebration, for baptism, ordination, blessing of the oil of the sick, and a prayer for burial. The prayer for the blessing of the people which we give here is notably relevant. Text in Funk, *Didascalia e Costituzioni Apostoliche,* Paderborn 1905, p. 164 (Euchologion 6, 29).

Baptismal liturgy. Attributed to Cyprian of Antioch. *Page 30.*

We have no certain biographical knowledge of Cyprian of Antioch, of whom a legend says he was a magician before his conversion. Two prayers are wrongly attributed to him, taken, however, from the works of Cyprian of Carthage. They probably derive from the ancient baptismal liturgy and are intended to dispose the heart to penitence and a plea for pardon from God before receiving the sacrament. We give here an excerpt from one of the prayers. The Latin text of this prayer, of which we give only sections, is in *Patrologia Latina* 4, 995-996.

Communion chant: Let us invoke Christ. *Page 32.*

In the form of a litany the chant repeats, underlines and exalts the love of Christ who gives himself in the Eucharist, the memorial of his immolation, after a whole life on earth offered in love and service. From a text studied and edited by N. Borgia (*Frammenti Eucaristici Antichissimi,* Grottaferrata 1932).

Communion chant: Your sacrament, Lord Jesus Christ. *Page 34.*

This eucharistic chant certainly goes back to the beginning of the 3rd century. It is identical in expression, rhythm and imagery with one extant in the apocryphal *Acts of Thomas* composed in the first half of the 3rd century. It is to be found in *Acta Apostolorum Apocrypha* edited by R. A. Lipsius and M. Bonnet, 1891-1903, vol. II, p. 268.

Communion chant: He has given them a heavenly bread. *Page 36.*

This chant is written on an ostrakon preserved in the *Collection of the Egypt Fund* (no. 101). It is incomplete. There are constant biblical allusions and its spirituality is notable. Its eucharistic content and its litanic form indicate that it was probably recited or chanted during or after communion. Critically studied and published by D. F. Cabrol and H. Leclercq in *Monumenta Ecclesiae Liturgica,* vol. I, p. ccxxxv.

Communion chant: You, who once spoke to Moses. *Page 38.*

Found on an ostrakon preserved in the Cairo Museum (No. 1856). It proceeds by parallel and antithesis to exalt the marvellous condescension of the Son of God who became incarnate among men. Studied and published by D. F. Cabrol and M. Leclercq, *op. cit.,* vol. II, p. ccxxxi.

Canticle for the Easter vigil. Today, we have contemplated. *Page 40.*

Canticle with eucharistic and paschal content repeatedly eschatological. It was studied and edited by N. Borgia, *op. cit.,* pp. 46-50.

Hymn for the Nativity: Sons of men. *Page 42.*

This hymn derives most probably from an ancient liturgy for the Nativity, of Eastern origin, as is borne out by the triple invocation to God as "Holy", peculiar to the prayers of the Eastern Church. The invocation applied to Christ is an explicit confession of his divinity. The hymn is to be found on an ostrakon in the National Museum in Brussels. It has been studied and published by D. F. Cabrol and M. Leclercq, *op. cit.,* p. ccxxxii.

Easter hymn: We glorify you, O Christ. *Page 44.*

The hymn, which is presumed to date back to the 3rd-4th century, is an acrostic on a fly-leaf, with six strophes each of four lines followed by a refrain. It is preserved in a 6th century papyrus from which the first strophe is certainly missing. It exalts Christ, born of the Holy Spirit and of the Virgin Mary, as the new Moses who saves lost people. It is kept in the John Rylands Library,

Manchester, and has been studied and published by D. F. Cabrol and M. Leclercq, *op. cit.*, vol. II, p. ccii.

To Christ the first-born. Anonymous hymn. *Page 46.*

This prayer-hymn seems to be a paraphrase of the first chapter of Paul's Letter to the Colossians in which he exalts Christ as Lord of the universe and of history. The text, mutilated, is found in a papyrus preserved in the collection of the Archduke Ranieri at Vienna. The numerous repetitions have been eliminated to make the meaning clearer. *Patrologia Orientale* (ed. Graffin and F. Nau) 18, 445-448.

Evening hymn. From a primitive liturgy. *Page 48.*

This hymn, still recited in the Evening Office of the Greek Church, seems to belong to an earlier date than the *Gloria* (the oldest codex containing the *Gloria,* the Codex Alexandrinus, dates back to the 5th century). Basil writes about this hymn in his tract on the Holy Spirit (29, 33): "Our fathers did not wish to receive the grace of the evening light in silence; as soon as it appeared, they blessed God. We do not know the name of the author of this hymn of thanksgiving, an ancient canticle which all the people continue to recite". The hymn presumably dates back to the 3rd-4th century. Text in W. Christ-M. Paranikas, *Anthologia Graeca Carminum Christianorum*, Lypsia 1871, p. 40.

Prayer to Christ. Egyptian epigraph. *Page 50.*

Many expressions of faith of the first Christian generations have come down to us in the form of an epigraph, which preserves in a personal and perhaps spontaneous form an ancient mode of prayer. These inscriptions on stone, belonging not to literature but to life, witness to faith in the Most Holy Trinity, in Christ and in the Holy Spirit. They are an auspicious prayer for the life above and beg for intercession with God. Placed on the tombs of the dead, these epigraphs were multiplied above all from the end of the 4th century, after the close of the persecutions. The greater number has been found in Egypt. The prayer in the form of a litany addressed to Christ, which we give here, in which there are evident references to primitive liturgical hymns, is carved on a sarcophagus found in a necropolis at Djebel Riha, between Aleppo and Alexandretta. Text in C. M. Kaufmann, *Handbuch der Altchristlichen Epigraphik*, Freiburg 1917, p. 151.

Prayer from the anaphora of Gregory. Coptic liturgy. *Page 52.*

The ancient Church of Egypt, later known as "Coptic" (i.e., Egyptian), numbers among its sons men of such spiritual calibre as Athanasius and Cyril; and it has the great merit of having kept alive and fervent even in Islamic surroundings, always hostile and often oppressive, for more than twelve centuries (from 640 to the beginning of the 19th century). Its liturgy, going back to the tradition of early Egyptian Christianity, is simpler in rite than others of the Eastern Churches. There are three forms: that most in use is that of Basil, the least used is that under the name of Cyril, and that of Gregory is reserved for solemnities. We give here the universal prayer to Christ from the anaphora taken from the liturgy of Gregory. Text in E. Renaudot, *Liturgiarum Orientalium Collectio*, Paris 1716, vol. I, p. 31.

Prayer before martyrdom. Afra of Augusta. *Page 54.*

We know little of the life of this young woman. According to her "passion" she was a public sinner. She was arrested while still a catechumen at the height of the Diocletian persecution, probably in the year 304. Condemned to the fire, she was burnt on a small island in the middle of a river running close to Augsburg (in Latin: Augusta) in federal Germany. From the midst of the flames her voice was heard giving thanks to Jesus Christ with the prayer which we here transcribe. Text in D. Ruinart, *Acta Primorum Martyrum Sincera*, 1959, pp. 482-484.

Hymn for Ascension day. Ephrem Syrus. *Page 56.*

Ephrem is the most eminent among the Syrian writers of the 4th and 5th centuries. Born at Nisibis in 306 (modern Nisaybin, in south-east Turkey) of a Christian family, he studied and taught in the city until it was conquered by the Persians in 363. He then moved to Edessa, in the Roman province of Syria, where he founded "the Persian school", so called because it was frequented by many Christians of Persian origin. There he taught until his death in 373. Of a contemplative soul, Ephrem gained from his studies and contacts with God a knowledge of the divine mysteries of which he sings in his works. His immense theological and poetical productivity earned him the title of "lyre of the Holy Spirit"; in fact, he exalts the beauty of faith in order to defend orthodoxy, and he instructs the faithful with his songs. His most sincere poetry is found in the *Songs of Nisibis*, a composition basically historical in which he narrates his country's misfortune during the Persian wars. His poetic works were soon translated by the Greeks who were rather poor in Christian poetry; and later had much influence on the Byzantine liturgy. This hymn is still in the Syriac Breviary (Various Hymns, 18). The text is to be found in Th. J. Lamy, *S. Efraem Syri et Sermones*, Malines 1902, vol. IV, pp. 748-750.

Prayer of an old man. Ephrem Syrus. *Page 58.*

According to the German translation given in *Bibliothek der Kirchenvater*, Kempten 1876, this prayer is taken from *Proverbs* (130).

Prayer to the suffering Christ. Ephrem Syrus. *Page 60.*

According to the German translation given in *Bibliothek der Kirchenvater*, Kempten 1876, this prayer is taken from the *Sermon on the Suffering of the Saviour* (9).

Paschal doxology. Gregory Nazianzen. *Page 62.*

Gregory (c. 330-389) was born in Nazianz in Cappadocia (the region in the east of Asia Minor belonging to Turkey) and was ordained at about the age of thirty by a tyrannical act of his father. Later, having become a bishop, he resigned his see almost at once, being bewildered by intrigues and complications of a practical character. Being drawn rather to meditation and the literary life than to action, he is known among the Greeks as the "theologian" or the "Christian Demosthenes" and his introverted and dissatisfied spirit is apparent in his homilies, discourses and poetry. With Basil and Gregory of Nyssa he formed a triad of luminaries of Cappadocia. From the doctrinal point of view the best part of his writings is contained in 45 discourses, among which those in defence of the doctrine of the Trinity are the most notable. 245 letters have also come down to us, together with some poems. His personal vicissitudes and acute sensibility give a special tone to Gregory's writings. He anticipates the *Confessions* of St Augustine. His prayers are so profoundly human that they make him extraordinarily modern. This paschal doxology ends the last discourse pronounced by Gregory just before his death. *Patrologia Graeca* 36, 664.

Hymn for the night. Gregory Nazianzen. *Page 64.*

Taken from his theological poems in *Patrologia Graeca* 27, 311-314.

Prayer in sickness. Gregory Nazianzen. *Page 66.*

Taken from his historical poems and collected on the basis of events which took place in the year 382. *Patrologia Graeca* 37, 1279-1280.

To the eternal creator of the world. Ambrose. *Page 68.*

Ambrose, bishop of Milan, is considered to be the creator of sacred hymnology in the West, having introduced the singing of hymns of his own composition into the liturgy. There was a flowering of hymns after this time which were generically known as Ambrosian although not all that have come down to us are his work. St Augustine attests the authenticity of four Ambrosian hymns among which is the Matins hymn "Aeterna Rerum Conditor" reproduced here. Text in *Patrologia Latina* 16, 1473.

Easter hymn. Asterius of Amasea. *Page 70.*

Asterius, bishop of Amasea in Pontus (†-c. 410) left various homilies full of life, inspired by scriptural and liturgical themes, or in praise of the martyrs and saints. The Easter hymn given here is to be found in *Patrologia Graeca* 40, 436 (XIX Homily on Psalm 5).

Hymn to Christ the light and life. Synesius of Cyrene. *Page 72.*

An aristocratic Libyan (?-c. 414) who is one of the strangest figures of Christian antiquity. Refined by the Greek culture he attained in the school of Alexandria, he was elected by popular enthusiasm bishop of Tolemaides even if, like Ambrose, he was not yet baptised. He undertook his pastoral office with zeal, but did not succeed in shaking off completely his former Greco-pagan culture. Besides tracts, sermons and letters, he has left some hymns in the Doric dialect which reveal, within a strange mixture of neo-Platonic ideas and Christian thought, a powerful genius and a vast knowledge. We give two excerpts from his hymns that exactly echo Platonic thought. Text in *Patrologia Graeca* 66, 1608-1609.

Evening hymn. Armenian liturgy. *Page 74.*

Evangelised at the dawn of the 4th century by Gregory the Illuminator, Armenia is notable in Christian history as the first nation to receive the Christian religion as a State religion (probably in 314). In its initial phase the Armenian liturgy stemmed from that of Caesarea, as did all other liturgies' evolutions, even that of the Byzantine liturgy. Today the Armenian rite is one of the five principal rites of the Eastern Church. The liturgy now in use dates back to the end of the 5th century, with later additions belonging to the 11th-16th centuries. We publish an Evening hymn composed before the 10th century which still forms part of the prayer of Vespers. It is reproduced by kind permission of Saris Sarkissan.

In praise of the Cross. Paulinus of Nola. *Page 76.*

Meropius Pontius Paulinus (352-431) was born of a patrician Roman family in Bordeaux (France). He was the favourite pupil of Ausonius (see hymn 53) and was successful in a political career, becoming Consul and Governor of Campania. Receiving baptism at Bordeaux in 396, he gave almost all his patrimony to the poor, and, with his wife's agreement, lived an austere, almost monastic life, first in Spain, where he was ordained priest, and then in Nola (Italy) near the tomb of St Felix (a saint of Syrian origin, bishop of this city for whom Paulinus built a basilica with what remained of his patrimony). He was consecrated bishop of Nola, governing it zealously until his death. Besides his correspondence with the most illustrious persons of his day, Paulinus left important poetic works, including the *Carmina natalicia* in honour of St Felix, and religious and occasional poetry. This hymn is taken from *Carmina* 19, 718-730. *Patrologia Latina* 61, 550.

Morning hymn. Prudentius. *Page 78.*

Marcus Aurelius Clement Prudentius (c. 348-c. 405) was a native of Calahorra in Spain, where he occupied important political and military posts. Towards the end of his life he retired into solitude to give himself up entirely to God and to poetry, in order to — as he wrote — expiate his faults. His poetic works, of true religious lyrical and didactic inspiration, put him in the first rank among Western Christian hymn writers. This hymn is to be found in *Cathemerinon Liber*. Text in the *Roman Breviary* (1960).

Preface for Epiphany. Ambrosian liturgy. *Page 80.*

The Sacramentaries are books which contain the prayer formulae of the first Christian assemblies and they offer a collection of Prefaces (the prayer which precedes the central portion of the eucharistic celebration). As with other prayers, initially the celebrant was allowed to compose the preface but later, with the birth of formulae composed for the purpose, it became practically fixed. The prefaces attributed in the various codices to the Ambrosian liturgy are about 300; the oldest (about 76 of them) are pre-6th century and plainly demonstrate their Milanese origin. They exhibit a richness in respect of the Roman and other Western liturgies. These prefaces, brief compositions which draw inspiration from the events of the Gospel or hagiography, unfold the praise of God for his good-ness, because "it is right and dutiful and the source of salvation". We give here the preface for the Epiphany and, following that for Easter. Text in A. Paredi, *I prefazi ambrosiani* 1937, p. 130.

Preface for Easter. Ambrosian liturgy. *Page 82.*

Text in A. Paredi, *I prefazi ambrosiani,* 1937, p. 148.

Canticle for the resurrection of Lazarus. Romanos the Melodious. *Page 84.*

Romanos, called "the Melodious", was a Syrian, of an Israelite family, born between 475 and 490. He died about 560 in Constantinople. He had settled there at about the age of twenty; was converted to Christianity and was ordained deacon. He served at the Church of the Virgin where he was buried after his death. Together with Sergius of Constantinople, Sophronius of Damascus and Andrew of Crete, he brought Greek hymnody to great prominence. Their odes and hymns and other compositions were rapidly assimilated into the Byzantine liturgy. Text in *Sources Chretiennes* 114-301.

Prayer for help. Pope Pelagius I. *Page 86.*

Pope Pelagius I was born in Rome at unknown date and died in 561. In 536 he was already a deacon, close to Pope Agapitus, in the unhappy years when the Church was under the heavy hand of the Emperor Justinian. When Rome was occupied by Totila, king of the Goths, Pelagius was present and confronted him, demanding clemency for the people. He was elected pope upon designation by the emperor, and this brought on him much adversity. However, during his brief pontificate he tried hard to bring the Roman clergy together again, to repair churches and to stimulate works of charity. He is buried in St Peter's. Text in *Patrologia Latina*, suppl. IV, 1275.

Hymn to the Cross. Venantius Fortunatus. *Page 88.*

Venantius Fortunatus, was born near Treviso in 540 and died at Poitiers in France a little after 600; he was bishop of that city. He was a court poet; then, being ordained priest, he became spiritual director of a monastic community of women. His culture brought him to know other learned men of his time. A great number of his poems, epitaphs, hymns and elegies, almost all of Christian inspiration, have come to us. Among his hymns the most well-known are the *Vexilla Regis prodeunt*, translated below, and the *Pange lingua*, still in use in the liturgy. Text in the *Roman Breviary* (1960).

Prayer to obtain forgiveness. Hibernian-Celtic hymnody. *Page 90.*

The Hibernian-Celtic hymnody forms part of the manifestations of barbaric cultures which developed in the area of Latin literature in Ireland and England at the height of the Middle Ages. In the Church of these regions many peni-tential books were written (minutely regulating the penances to be applied to different sins) and it is from this atmosphere, with its sense of sin and widespread penitential spirit, that we cull the following prayer. Text in *Patrologia Latina*, suppl. IV, 2075.

Prayer for salvation. Maximus. *Page 92.*

Maximus, saint and confessor (580-652), was born at Constantinople and dedicated himself to serious study, especially of philosophy. He was called to the imperial court to fill the post of first secretary, but abandoned it at the age of 34 to become a monk. Persecuted by the supporters of heresy, imprisoned, tortured and mutilated in the tongue and arm, he was finally sent into exile in the region of Batum (to the east of the Black Sea) where he died after two years. He left about sixty volumes of exegesis and ascetical writing. Text in *Patrologia Graeca* 91, 1422-1425.

Christmas prayer. Mozarabic liturgy. *Page 94.*

Its name derives from the adjective meaning "to be made arabic", and was given by the Arabs, during their occupation, to Christian Spaniards. The liturgy, however, in spite of this adjective, is Western in essence. It is also called Visigothic or Hispanic. Originally it drew from the Latin literary culture of the Spain of the 7th and 8th centuries, continuing to the end of the 12th. Dense in concepts and expressed in a sumptuous rite, it is now preserved only in the Cathedral of Toledo.

Lenten hymn. The Venerable Bede. *Page 96.*

Bede, saint and doctor of the Church (673-735), English like Alcuin, is considered, if not the greatest, one of the most learned men of the Middle Ages. At the age of 7 he was offered to a monastery and remained there until his death. The major part of his work consists of biblical exegesis. The better part of his work, considered from the stylistic and literary point of view, consists in historical works, in particular the history of the Anglosaxon Church. Venerated as a saint soon after his death, he was proclaimed doctor of the Church by Pope Leo XIII. Text in *Patrologia Latina*, suppl. IV, 2239.

Prayer for the catholic Church. Alcuin's Liturgical Collection. *Page 98.*

Alcuin, born in England about 735, died at Tours in France in 1804. Of a noble Anglosaxon family, he was a disciple of the Archbishop of York. He was ordained deacon and given charge of the "Schola" (the first university of that city), whose prestige and fame he augmented. During a mission to Rome he met the Emperor Charlemagne at Parma, who persuaded him, under vigorous pressure, to stay with him as counsellor. In a short time he became the emperor's preceptor in all the sciences. His culture in fact was multiform, and his vast literary output ranged from philosophy and theology to history and rules of poetry. As an outstanding member of the French liturgical school he resisted the acceptance of Roman liturgical books. We give a prayer to Christ from the *Liturgical Collection* which bears his name. Text in *Patrologia Latina* 101, 487ff.

Thanksgiving to Jesus. Gallican Formularies. *Page 100.*

In classical antiquity a form of literary composition was known which consisted in collecting together passages in prose and verse and phrases of well known authors, and was called "patch-work". This literary exercise was also practised by the Christians of the first centuries who made a "patch-work" of prayers, homilies and treatises from the first Fathers, thus composing formulae for prayer in the community assembly. Substantially these prayer formulae were of individual inspiration, due to the celebrant or his assistants or a versed lay person. They varied from Church to Church, and when they became common, were collected in codices called formularies. Today these formularies are precious for the history of liturgy. Text in *Patrologia Latina* 101, 477ff.

Ode to Christ the saviour. Cosmas of Maiuma. *Page 102.*

The Laura of St Sabas, consisting of a group of anchorites living separately but under the authority of a superior, arose in the rocky desert between Jerusalem and the Dead Sea. Famous among them was John Damascene. Cosmas was his adopted brother, and was a simple monk in the "laura". In 743 he became bishop of Maiuma. In collaboration with other writers among the anchorites and especially with John Damascene he composed the *Octoechos* (an Office containing the hymns for the Sundays of the Year in the Byzantine liturgy). Text in *Octoechos*, Rome 1886.

Ode to Christ crucified. Byzantine liturgy. *Page 104.*

The Byzantine rite, more than any other Christian rite, reserves a very special place for the cult of the cross. The liturgical books of the Byzantine Church overflow with hymns, generally short, referring to the cross and Christ crucified. The texts were composed by the Eastern Fathers from the 6th to the 9th centuries. To us, far away from the Eastern mentality, and generally given to expressing our faith in a measured and detached way, the warmth of this expression of praise may seem too much for our prayer. Text in Sr. Maria, *La Croce nella Preghiera Bizantina*, Brescia 1979, p. 88.

Plea for protection. Gregory of Narek. *Page 106.*

The period of the great cultural progress in Armenia, known as the first Armenian renaissance, and dating from the end of the 9th century, saw the emergence into the poetry of religion and liturgy of the mystic Gregory, a monk of the city of Narek. He lived from 951 to 1003 (or 1010) and in the silence of his monastery developed a natural capacity for listening and for loftiness. His lyrics are full of his anxiety over the social reality of the time and the suffering of the people living through it. His book of elegies, commonly called the *Narek*, can be considered as his masterpiece; he is also the author of panegyrics, odes and hymns. After the Bible, the *Narek* was the most read book in Armenia, because, in spite of the difficulty in penetrating into its full meaning, the people were able to discern in it something they already saw reflected in their soul. Text in *Sources Chretiennes*, 7, p. 522.

Prayer to Christ the creator. Gregory of Narek. *Page 108.*
Text in *Sources Chretiennes*, 78, p. 523.

Index of Headings

125

Stampa:
Istituto Grafico Bertello - 1982
Printed in Italy